First published in USA 1995 by Collins Publishers San Francisco
Copyright © 1995 by Collins Publishers San Francisco
Recipes and text copyright © 1995 Edon Waycott
Photographs copyright © 1995 Kathryn Kleinman
Food Stylist: Stephanie Greenleigh
Floral and Prop Stylist: Michaele Thunen
Art Direction and Design: Jennifer Barry
Series Editor: Meesha Halm
Library of Congress Cataloging-in-Publication Data
Waycott, Edon.
Summer fruit: a country garden cookbook / by Edon Waycott;
photography by Kathryn Kleinman.
p. cm.
Includes index.
ISBN 0-00-255451-8
1. Cookery (Fruit) I. Title
TX811.W33 1995
641.6'4—dc20 CIP 94-40214
Printed in China
1 3 5 7 9 10 8 6 4 2

Acknowledgments

Nature has a plan for all her fruits. If we observe this plan, we will
reap abundant rewards. Fruit that has been allowed to ripen and
sweeten on the tree tastes the way nature wanted it to. I am grateful
to all the farmers who adhere to this simple and modest premise and
are not coerced into sacrificing inherent flavor for mass production
or shipping properties. Special thanks to the farmers who are now
returning to heirloom varieties of fruits and growing them without
chemical pesticides or fertilizers, and to those who so willingly
shared information with me at the Santa Monica farmers' market.

Thanks also to Meesha Halm, who guided this book with insight,
vision and creative encouragement and was always a helpful and
astute editor.

Time in the kitchen is rarely time alone: I have a wonderful
husband who not only tastes and critiques everything I cook, but
who also does the dishes.

Collins and the photography team would also like to thank Terry
Greene, Kirstie Laird, Eric Schwab, Helga Sigvaldadottir and
Rachel Weill, photography assistants; Cachet Bean, production
assistant; Patricia Brill and Claudia Breault, food-styling assis-
tants; Assumpta Curry, design and production coordinator, and
Susan Swant, manufacturing manager. Thanks also to Candy
Overman; Tony Calabrese of Calabrese Farms in Brentwood;
Michael Bates in Santa Rosa and Bob Knuth, for their help on
location, and Ray Giacopazzi of Hillcrest Gardens in Petaluma.
Thanks to Manderly in San Rafael, the Jimtown Store in
Healdsburg, Pavillion Antiques in San Anselmo, Barbara Hoopes,
and Jenny Barry for their props. Also, to Svetlana Darche,
Sunnyside Nursery in San Anselmo, and Mary and Hank
McKowen for their generous donation of summer fruit. Finally,
special thanks to Susan Hastings and Hans Nehme, Ed Haverty,
and Michael, Eric and Peter Schwab.

CONTENTS

INTRODUCTION

For generations, fruit has been grown and sold because it is delicious. Profit and nourishment came second to taste, which you could pretty much guarantee would be sensational merely by leaving the fruit on the tree until it was ready to eat. Juice stains and sticky fingers from plucking a really ripe plum and devouring it among low-hanging branches humming with bees were among the pleasures of summer. So was the joy of finding a perfect peach on the ground, unblemished and warm, lying in the tall grass where the mower hadn't reached. Very probably, the fruit was grown on your own or a neighboring plot of land and your grandmother would spend weeks at the stove, canning and preserving great quantities for the winter months. Picked ripe and marketed locally, the varieties didn't travel far.

I didn't grow up with apricots, plums or nectarines, but I did grow up with peaches. And it was the peach that caused me to be forever crazy about the stone fruits of summer. The first peach pie or cobbler of the season was always the best, and we never had a Fourth of July without peach ice cream made in that squeaky hand-cranked machine. Mother put up spiced (she called them "pickled") Elberta peaches, which appeared at winter dinners on a white, oval ironstone platter with baked ham. Peach jam, which turned a deep amber during cooking, reminded us of summer as we slathered it on toast in January. But the beautiful Georgia Belle peaches, blushing debutantes, were the most coveted. Not daring to adulterate their pristine pale flesh and crimson centers, we always ate them fresh. Cecil Webb grew the best peaches in the county where my grandparents lived. We would buy them by the half-bushel from his roadside stand. Their heady aroma would fill the humid Southern summer air; their downy skin would invite a caress. Larger than tennis balls, there were disappointingly few in each basket.

Summer stone fruits are a little like houseguests: They don't tiptoe in. Instead, they shout their arrival and dump an enormous amount of all-ripe-at-once produce on your doorstep. And just when you begin to feel complacent about their presence or start being creative in the kitchen, they disappear, and one of their cousins arrives. And so it goes until after Labor Day.

The first to show up are the fat burgundy Bing and Lambert cherries, which appear in late May. They are soon followed by other members of the cherry family: sweet Royal Ann, golden Rainier, and the tart Montmorency and Morello. Although cherries are grown all over the world, the United States is the largest producer. The Bing cherry, ideal for eating out of hand, was developed in 1875 in Oregon and has now become the variety most commonly grown in Washington and California. Tart or sour cherries, used for cooking or preserving, account for almost two-thirds of this country's crop; the majority come from Michigan, Wisconsin and New York state.

The nectarine's arrival overlaps the cherry's, and its season extends well into August. Often mistakenly thought to be a cross between a peach and a plum, the nectarine is a variety of peach with a smooth, fuzzless skin. Originally from China, the nectarine has found a welcome place on our summer menus. There are thousands of varieties, with the delicate white-fleshed ones considered the best.

The apricot season is all too short. When I first moved to California, I had a tree in the backyard, and it seemed as if every apricot ripened on the same day. Until recently, fresh apricots were unknown in several regions of the United States and accounted for only a small percentage of sales; the bulk of the fruit was sold dried. Fortunately for the consumer, that meager percentage has now tripled. Due to a new and better-tasting variety called Castlebrite, which is also a good shipper, the golden fruit now travels well and far. Generally, the deeper the color, the sweeter the apricot.

Although originally from China, the peach was brought to the New World in the 1600s by Spanish explorers from Persia, where it had been cultivated for centuries. One hundred years later Catholic missionaries planted the fruit in California, and now that state accounts for fifty percent of domestic production. For many, the onset of peach season signals the beginning of summer. It is a grand excuse for making ice cream and pies and for dressing up cereal and breakfast drinks. Peaches have inspired poets, artists and, quite naturally, cooks. Peach Melba, the unmistakably French dessert, was created by the great Auguste Escoffier for the Australian soprano Dame Nellie Melba.

By late July the fruit bins at farmers' markets form a palette of colors, from crimson to deep purple to a pale yellow-green. Plums, which vary in size and shape from the small elongated Italian variety to the giant black Friar, can be divided into two categories: European plums, brought to America in colonial times, and Japanese plums, introduced to this continent around 1870. Most of the plums we see now are the larger Japanese variety, which are primarily sold fresh. Prunes are usually made from European plums, which have a high sugar content and will not ferment if the pit is left in while drying.

Any of the darker-skinned plums can be turned into a great jam. If the variety is naturally sweet and ripe, they need very little sugar, and since their skins break down and thicken the juices, you will not need to add any pectin. The sweetness of the pulp and tartness of the skin creates a fine counter-point. Cooked down to a concentrated intensity, plums combine equally well with sweet or savory elements in tarts, barbecue sauces or salads.

Over the years, much of the flavor has been bred out of commercial produce in order for it to have better shipping, storing and disease-resistant qualities. Sometimes the only clues to discovering the variety is the fruit's shape and color. But recently small growers have been inspired to return to heirloom varieties, which taste more like what you may remember savoring on your grandmother's back porch. If the fruit is pesticide-free, it may not look as perfect as a supermarket variety, but it will have a far better aroma and taste. The best sources of such wonderful fruit are a grower's roadside stand, a local farmers' market, or, perhaps most economical, U-Pick farms and orchards. Take the kids, baskets in hand, and make a day of it. You will develop a new standard for judging taste after pulling a ripe apricot or plum from a tree, wiping the dust off on your shirt, and biting into the warm, juicy fruit.

Even though these stone fruits of summer have common characteristics that allow them to be easily interchanged and combined, they are each unique. Appreciate their differences and indulge in their similarities. But above all, find fruit that has stayed on the tree long enough that you can identify it by its aroma with your eyes closed.

GLOSSARY

Stone fruits are simply ones that contain a single pit or "stone." They are generally classified as either "freestone," in which the flesh is easily separated from the pit, "clingstone," in which the flesh clings to the pit, and "semi-freestone." The most common summer fruit are apricots, cherries, nectarines, peaches and plums. All are members of the genus *Prunus*. High in vitamins A and C, they range in calories from approximately 20 for an apricot to 85 for a nectarine.

Availability: Apricots are in season from June through August, cherries from late May to August, nectarines from June through September, peaches from June through October, and plums from June through October.

Selecting:

Apricots: Apricots should be intensely orange and fairly firm. Fruit tinged with pale yellow or green will not ripen after purchase. Most are freestone; the remainder are classified as semi-freestone.

Cherries: Sweet cherries should be dark red or golden skinned and firm to the touch. Sour cherries are scarlet to light red. All varieties should be free of blemishes and have green stems, which indicate freshness.

Nectarines: Nectarines should have an orange-red background color. They should yield to gentle pressure but not be as soft as peaches. Nectarines fall into two categories: freestone and clingstone.

Peaches: Peaches should have a creamy or golden background color and yield to gentle pressure. The red blush on a peach does not indicate ripeness. Once picked, peaches will ripen but not increase in sweetness. Peaches, like nectarines, are either freestone or clingstone. They can have yellow or white flesh.

Plums: Plums vary in color, so choose ones that are full-colored for their variety. Avoid fruit with blemished or broken skin or with a brown discoloration at the stem end. The light-skinned plums are quite firm.

Storing:

Apricots: Ripen apricots at room temperature, then store in the refrigerator, where they will keep for several days. For best flavor bring them to room temperature before eating.

Cherries: Highly perishable, cherries should not be washed until they are ready to be used. Keep them in the refrigerator on paper towel–lined plates in one layer.

Nectarines and Peaches: These fruits may be ripened for 2 or 3 days at room temperature, then stored for up to a week in the refrigerator.

Plums: Plums may be ripened at room temperature for 2 or 3 days, then stored in the refrigerator for up to 3 days.

Preparing:

To pit a freestone fruit, simply cut in half vertically along the natural indentation, from flower end to stem end. Twist the halves apart and lift out the pit.

A semi-freestone or clingstone fruit will rarely fall from its pit. The easiest way to remove the flesh is to vertically cut the desired number of slices into the pit, turning the fruit to cut all the way around. The slices can then be pulled away. Some flesh will remain on the pit.

Cooking:

Apricots: Since their flesh falls away from the pit and their skins do not have to be removed, apricots are extremely easy to prepare. They cook down to a velvety smooth jam and make tangy additions to mixed fruit cobblers and pies. Home-dried apricots are very dark; commercially dried fruit contains small amounts of sulfur dioxide, used to retain the color. Good flavor enhancers include orange juice, cinnamon and nutmeg.

Cherries: Cherries are easily pitted with an inexpensive gadget called a cherry (or olive) pitter. Choose one that does not flatten the cherry during the operation. Usually, sweet cherries are eaten fresh and sour cherries are used for jams and pies. There's no harm in cooking sweet cherries, but they are not as juicy and will require less sugar than the tart varieties. Good flavor enhancers are almond, cinnamon and nutmeg.

Nectarines and Peaches: Peaches are easily peeled by plunging them into rapidly boiling water for 1 minute. Remove to a bowl of ice water for easier handling, then pull off the skin after making a nick with the tip of a paring knife. You do not need to peel nectarines. To prevent the fruit from darkening after slicing, sprinkle with lemon juice. Peaches and nectarines can almost always be interchanged. The yellow-fleshed fruits are better suited for baking and preserving since they darken during cooking. The white-fleshed varieties are best fresh or lightly poached.

Plums: Found in more varieties than almost any other fruit, plums offer an incredible range of flavors. The dark-skinned ones with either red or yellow flesh make wonderful jam. No peeling is necessary; the skins dissolve and thicken the juices naturally. All varieties are good for eating fresh and for cooking, except for the small Blue Damson, which is very tart and makes excellent preserves. Good flavor enhancers are cinnamon, cardamom, ginger and port wine.

Measurements and Equivalents:

1 pound of fruit equals:

8 to 12 apricots

3 to 5 medium peaches

3 to 5 medium nectarines

5 to 8 medium plums

3 cups unpitted cherries

There are hundreds of stone fruit cultivars; plums in particular come in a bewildering variety of colors, sizes and flavors. Because of pronounced differences, it is important to remember the names of favorites in order to ask for them again. The following selection spans cultivars available in different regions of the country and are suitable for a variety of purposes, from eating fresh to cooking and preserving.

Apricots:

Blenheim (also called Royal Blenheim and Royal): Medium to large pale orange fruit with red dots. Very juicy freestone flesh. Sweet, aromatic flavor that sets the standard for apricots. Famous in California for its good canning quality; also good for drying. Ripens in early July.

Castlebrite: Large, bright orange fruit with tart, firm flesh. Ships well. Best for cooking. Ripens in early July.

Katy: Medium to large bright yellow fruit. Semi-freestone. Good flavor. Best for canning, jams and cobblers. Ripens early, in the first week of June.

Moorpark: Very large fruit. Smooth, fuzzless, deep yellow skin with an orange-red blush. Juicy, sweet flesh. Excellent quality. Good for eating fresh, canning and drying. Good shipper as well. Long ripening period can extend from early July to late August.

Rival: Large symmetrical fruit. Light orange skin develops a pronounced red blush. Firm, fine-textured, deep orange flesh with a mild, low-acid flavor. Grown mainly in Washington state. Best eaten fresh. Available early in the season, usually in June.

Cherries:

Sweet

Bing: Large, heart-shaped, freestone fruit with dark red to brownish purple skin. Firm, meaty purple flesh. The leading commercial sweet cherry in the western United States, it is the cherry most commonly eaten fresh. Usually the first cherry variety to appear in the markets in late May; in some areas the season extends to early July.

Lambert: Sweet, dark red, heart-shaped fruit, slightly smaller than a Bing. Good fresh or cooked. Ripens from late June to early July.

Royal Ann: Very old French variety. Large light yellow fruit with a beautiful rose blush. Firm, juicy, sweet flesh. Excellent fresh and for canning. Often used for commercial maraschino cherries. Ripens mid-June to mid-July.

Rainier: Large yellow fruit with a red blush and firm, clear to light yellow flesh. Fine texture, distinct flavor. Colorless juice. Lacks the acidity to be a good cooking cherry, but has good storage properties. Ripens mid-June to mid-July.

Sour

Montmorency: The standard cherry for pies or jam. Medium large, bright red fruit with firm yellow flesh and clear juice. Rich, tart, tangy flavor. Doesn't get mushy during processing. Excellent for drying. Originated in France in the 17th century; introduced to the United States in 1760. Most commonly available fresh in the northern Midwest. Trees require a long chilling period to produce fine fruit. Ripens in late June.

Morello: Medium-sized reddish black pie cherry with semifirm, tart flesh and dark juice. Astringent until fully ripe. Originated in England. Best for canning and baking. Ripens in August and hangs on the tree until the end of August.

Nectarines:

Arctic Rose: Medium-sized, red to gold skin, white flesh. Recently has become more common in supermarkets because it resists bruising and can be shipped when quite ripe. Best eaten fresh to appreciate the delicate flavor and texture. Available for just a short season; ripens mid- to late August.

Fantasia: Large, egg-shaped freestone fruit with very smooth skin. Three-quarters bright red overlaid on brilliant yellow. Firm, smooth-textured yellow flesh of excellent quality. Can be harvested firm-ripe and tangy for shipping, or soft-ripe and sweet for local markets. Good for all purposes. Ripens in late June or first week of July.

Flavortop: Medium to large egg-shaped fruit; mostly red over a bright yellow background. Firm, smooth-textured, yellow freestone flesh of excellent quality. Ships well. Good for all purposes. Ripens in mid-July.

Independence: Large oval fruit is almost completely dark red. Firm, yellow freestone flesh. Rich tangy-sweet flavor. Best for preserves and pies. Ripens in early July in central California.

Le Grand: One of the first nectarines to appear in supermarkets. Large, very red skin with juicy yellow flesh. Good for eating fresh or baking. Ripens in early July.

Snow Queen: European white-fleshed nectarine of exceptional quality. Large, with blush red to rose skin with firm, delicate flesh. Sweet, intense flavor that is somewhat diminished in cooking. Perfect sliced in fresh fruit tarts, where the contrast of skin and flesh are visible. Ripens in early July.

Peaches:

Babcock: Medium-sized round fruit; almost fuzzless skin slightly blushed with red. Firm, juicy, white semi-freestone flesh turns red around the pit. Sweet flavor, aromatic. Not good for jam because it does not retain its pure color during long cooking. Beautiful poached or sliced in tarts. Ripens from late June to July.

Elberta: Most popular peach variety in America. Large yellow fruit with a crimson blush. Juicy, yellow freestone flesh. A leading high-quality, commercial-processing peach and a good shipper. Excellent for various desserts, canning and jam. Ripens from late July to early August.

Flavorcrest: Medium-sized round fruit, approximately two-thirds red at maturity. Exceptionally firm, yellow semi-freestone flesh. Ships well. Good for preserves and canning. Ripens in early July.

Georgia Belle: Old-time favorite. Large creamy white fruit with a bright red cheek. Firm white freestone flesh tinged with red. Highly flavored and aromatic. Bruises easily, so it

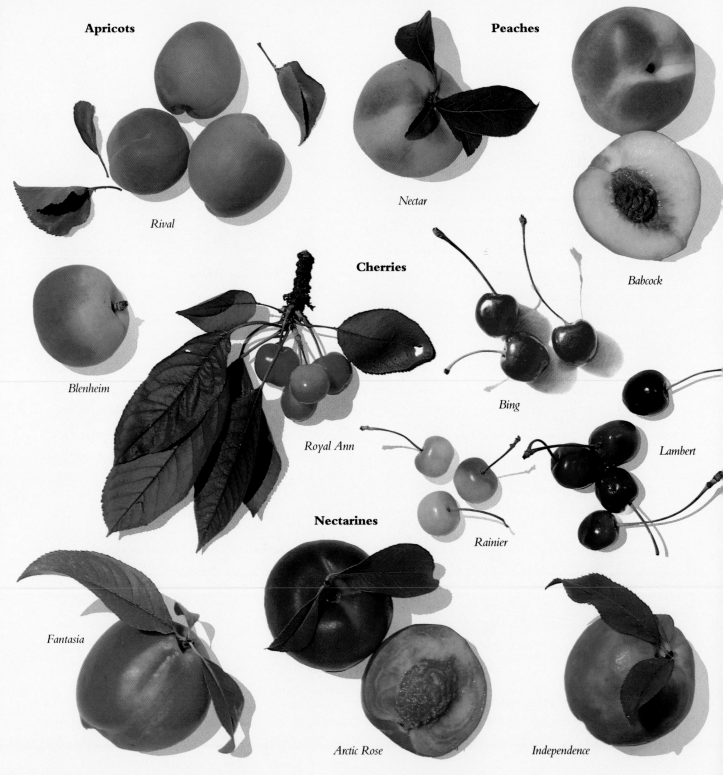

Apricots

Peaches

Rival

Nectar

Babcock

Cherries

Blenheim

Bing

Lambert

Royal Ann

Rainier

Nectarines

Fantasia

Arctic Rose

Independence

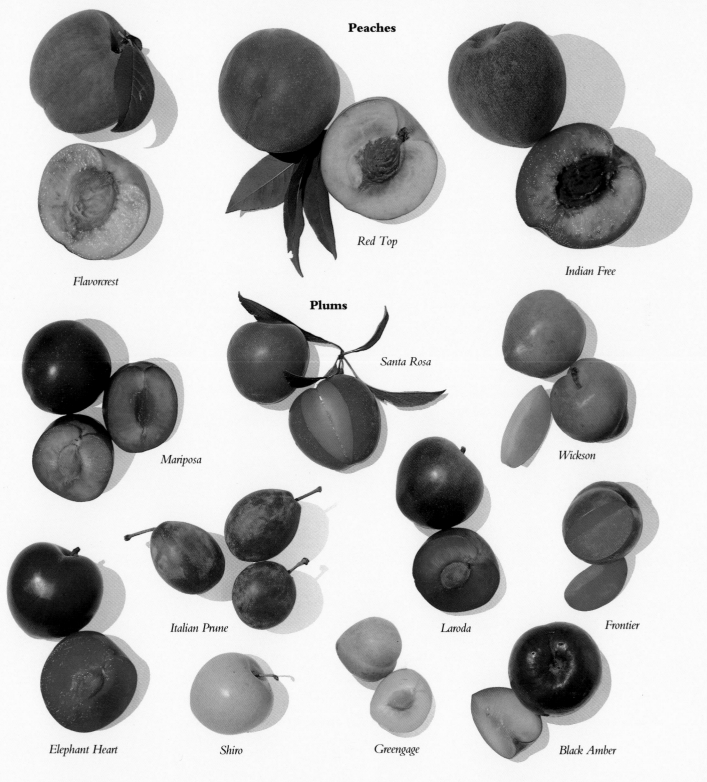

Peaches

Flavorcrest

Red Top

Indian Free

Plums

Santa Rosa

Mariposa

Wickson

Italian Prune

Laroda

Frontier

Elephant Heart

Shiro

Greengage

Black Amber

does not get shipped beyond the southeastern United States. Originated in Georgia around 1870. Best eaten fresh, but also makes wonderful ice cream. Ripens in early August.

Indian Free: Large, freestone fruit with firm red flesh. Tart until fully ripe; then becomes rich and sweet with distinctive flavor. Excellent fresh or for canning. Ripens in mid-August.

J.H. Hale: An old variety and still one of the best. Exceptionally large and round; freestone fruit is golden yellow overlaid with carmine. Skin is smooth and almost fuzzless. Firm, fine-grained deep yellow flesh is not stringy or mealy. Delicious flavor. Good for canning and fresh eating. Also an outstanding handling and shipping peach. Ripens in late July.

Nectar: Medium to large cream-colored fruit with dark pink blush. White freestone flesh with great taste, aroma and texture. Susceptible to bruising when ripe, so mostly available at local farmers' markets. Good for eating fresh and for making preserves. Ripens in late June.

O'Henry: Considered by many to be the best peach for taste and handling. Yellow flesh with good taste if allowed to ripen sufficiently. Most common peach in supermarkets. Better for cooking purposes. Ripens from the end of July into August.

Redtop: Smallish oval fruit with mostly yellow skin turning to blush. Freestone, with firm yellow flesh. Also commonly found in supermarkets. Good for pies and preserves. Ripens in early July.

Plums:

Angelina: Old English variety. Bluish, almost black, skin with yellowish green flesh and a rich, sweet flavor. Stays firm even when ripe. Very good for eating fresh. Ripens mid-July to mid-August.

Black Amber: Japanese plum. Round, firm, dark purple fruit with amber flesh. Very good for eating fresh and for cooking. Ripens in mid-July.

Blue Damson: A European plum. Small to medium-sized oval fruit. Bluish purple skin and tart, juicy golden yellow flesh. Excellent for jam and canning. Ripens from August to September.

Elephant Heart: Large, heart-shaped Japanese plum with thick bronze-green skin that turns reddish purple when completely ripe. Juicy, blood-red freestone flesh. Rich, distinctive flavor. Beautiful sliced fresh for tarts and other desserts. Ripens over a 14-day period in mid-July.

Friar: Large, round, dark purple Japanese plum that turns almost black when fully mature. Firm amber freestone flesh. Good quality. Tart skin and sweet flesh yield jam with good flavor and intense color. Ripens in August.

Frontier: Very dark Japanese plum with purple skin and a tinge of pale green. Large fruit with deep red flesh. Very good balance between tart skin and sweet, soft flesh. Makes wonderful, thick red jam. Ripens mid-July.

Greengage: European variety. Small to medium-sized oval, yellowish green fruit. Juicy, smooth-textured, amber flesh. Rich, sugary flavor. Good cooked, canned or preserved whole. Ripens in late June.

Italian Prune: European variety. Oval, medium-sized to large purplish black fruit. Juicy, greenish yellow, freestone flesh turns red when cooked. Distinctive, rich, sweet flavor. Good for canning, baking and drying. Ripens from August to September.

Laroda: Dark red, almost black, Japanese plum covered with tiny light dots. Pale violet-red flesh, yellow near the stone. Rich winelike flavor. Good for eating fresh or for making preserves. Ripens in August.

Mariposa: Large Japanese plum with pink to light purple juicy, nearly freestone flesh surrounding a small pit. Sweet, rich flavor. Excellent fresh or cooked. Ripens in mid-July.

Mirabelle: Small round fruit with yellow skin and yellow dots. Not beautiful, but sweet, firm, yellow freestone flesh. Good for jams, tarts and canning. Widely grown and highly esteemed in Europe, especially in France, where it is made into a brandy of the same name. Sometimes available in specialty markets in America. Ripens in late August.

President: European variety. Large, round to oblong, blue-black fruit. Fine-textured yellow freestone flesh. Good commercial variety. Not sweet enough for eating fresh; best for cooking. Keeps and ships well. Last of the plums to mature, this ripens from early to mid-September.

Santa Rosa: Very large, round to oval Japanese plum with purplish red fruit covered with light dots and a thin bloom. Fragrant, juicy, fine-textured clingstone flesh is purplish near the skin, yellow streaked with pink near the pit. Superb quality. Excellent fresh or canned. Keeps and ships well. Ripens in mid-July.

Satsuma: Small to medium, nearly round Japanese plum with dark red fruit and a small pit. Sweet, meaty, juicy red flesh. Wonderful for eating fresh or cooking and preserving. Ripens in late August.

Shiro: Medium to large, round Japanese plum with yellow fruit and a pink blush. Juicy, translucent yellow clingstone flesh. Mild, sweet flavor. Excellent for eating fresh, cooking, canning and for making preserves and desserts. Ripens in July.

Wickson: Large heart-shaped Japanese plum with greenish yellow fruit. Firm, very sweet translucent flesh. Very popular for eating fresh. Ripens in early August.

OPENERS

It's hard to improve on a piece of fruit. What nature has given, unadorned and uncooked, is already near perfect. Still, the overflowing fruit bowl of summer beckons every time you pass and prods you to devise ways to enjoy these luscious foods. How can you resist creating a dish around that smooth red nectarine? Or that purple plum with sweet amber flesh? The varieties of fruit are so numerous and the combinations so infinite that you can't let a meal go by without incorporating a few.

Begin your day by pouring warm, Chunky Apricot Maple Syrup over waffles or French toast. In early June, when the first cherries are in the markets, you can look forward to treating your family to tangy, light pancakes with Sweet Cherries in Pomegranate Syrup.

The first course is the perfect venue for uncooked assemblies of summer fruit augmented by simple dressings or balanced by a few well-chosen ingredients. For a festive play of Asian flavors try Plum and Ginger Salad, where the soothing plum tames the pungent ginger. Fruit Salsa with Spicy Pita Chips makes a light, palate-stimulating beginning to an outdoor barbecue. Puréed nectarines replace much of the oil in a vinaigrette while adding sweetness to Arugula and Sweet Onion Salad. A simple watermelon syrup drenches a cool fruit salad that awakens your taste buds.

Toasted Pecan Waffles with Chunky Apricot Maple Syrup

*These waffles have a substantial texture but are light in weight. Their nutty flavor
and interior crunch are a perfect match for the syrup, which combines the faint tartness of apricots
with the fragrant hominess of maple syrup. The syrup, which keeps refrigerated for 2 weeks, is also
delicious over ice cream. You can substitute peaches for some or all of the apricots,
but squeeze in a little lemon to offset their sweetness.*

Chunky Apricot Maple Syrup:
10 apricots
1 cup pure maple syrup
1 high-quality, moist, supple vanilla bean ★

1/2 cup pecans, finely chopped
1 1/2 cups all-purpose flour

1/4 cup cornmeal, preferably white
2 teaspoons baking powder
1 teaspoon baking soda
1/4 teaspoon salt
2 large eggs
1 1/2 cups buttermilk
6 tablespoons unsalted butter, melted

To make the syrup, pit 6 of the apricots and purée them in a food processor or blender.

In a small saucepan over medium heat, bring the maple syrup to a simmer and stir in the purée. Slit the vanilla bean lengthwise and scrape the seeds into the syrup mixture. Cut the pod into thirds and add to the syrup. Continue to simmer for 10 minutes, or until the syrup thickens slightly.

Just before serving, remove the bean pod. Pit and thinly slice the remaining apricots and add to the mixture. The syrup will thicken a little if allowed to cool to room temperature before serving. *Makes 2 cups of syrup*

Preheat the oven to 350 degrees F. and preheat a waffle iron.

Spread the pecans on a baking sheet and toast in the oven for 10 minutes. Set aside to cool.

In a large mixing bowl, stir together the cooled pecans, flour, cornmeal, baking powder, baking soda and salt. Add the eggs, buttermilk and butter and stir until the batter is smooth. Pour approximately 3/4 cup of batter onto the waffle iron and cook according to the manufacturer's instructions. Serve hot with the syrup. *Makes six 8-inch waffles*

★Note: High-quality vanilla beans are supple and moist, not dried out like most of those you find in supermarkets. Look for moist vanilla beans in specialty markets. Store them tightly wrapped in plastic in the refrigerator for up to 6 months.

Whole Wheat Yogurt Pancakes
with Sweet Cherries in Pomegranate Syrup

*These pancakes are soft and light without added egg whites, but if they are a little too lofty
for you, thin the batter with a tablespoon or two of milk. I buy pomegranate juice from a wonderful
lady at my local farmers' market who makes it with her apple press, but you can also find it bottled in Middle
Eastern markets. Warmed slightly, the sauce is delicious over ice cream or French toast.*

Sweet Cherries in Pomegranate Syrup:
4 cups pomegranate juice
1 cinnamon stick, approximately 3 inches in length
1/2 pound dark sweet cherries, pitted
1/2 cup loosely packed light brown sugar
1 teaspoon pure vanilla extract
2 teaspoons fresh lemon juice
*1 tablespoon cornstarch dissolved in 2 tablespoons
    cold water*

1 cup plain low-fat yogurt
1 large egg
3 tablespoons unsalted butter, melted
1/4 cup all-purpose flour
1/2 cup whole wheat flour
1/2 teaspoon salt
1 teaspoon baking soda
Unsalted butter, for greasing

To make the syrup, in a shallow pan over high heat, combine the pomegranate juice and cinnamon stick and bring to a boil. Continue cooking over high heat for approximately 30 minutes, or until the mixture is reduced by half.

Remove the cinnamon stick and add the cherries, brown sugar, vanilla, lemon juice and dissolved cornstarch. Return the mixture to a boil and continue to cook, stirring, for 5 minutes, or until the cherries look glazed and the syrup is thickened. Remove from the heat and let cool slightly before serving. The syrup can be stored covered in the refrigerator for 1 week. *Makes approximately 4 cups of syrup*

To make the pancakes, in a medium-sized mixing bowl, whisk together the yogurt, egg and butter. In a small bowl, stir together the flours, salt and baking soda. Add the dry ingredients to the yogurt mixture all at once and stir just until moistened; the batter will be lumpy.

Preheat the oven to the warm setting or 200 degrees F. Preheat a griddle or large skillet over moderately high heat. Lightly film the surface with butter and pour out approximately 1/4 cup of batter per pancake. Cook until bubbles break on the surface, then turn over and cook briefly on the other side. Keep the pancakes warm in the oven until all the batter is used. Serve with the warm Pomegranate Syrup. *Makes eight 4-inch pancakes*

Chilled Summer Fruit Salad in Watermelon Syrup

Watermelon is the quintessential symbol of summer. Because of its high water content and delicate taste and color, it is better eaten in as pure a form as possible. An exception is in this refreshing syrup, ideal for a fruit combination that doubles as a salad or dessert.

1/4 cup water
1/4 cup granulated sugar
2 tablespoons coarsely chopped fresh mint
2-pound piece of watermelon (weighed with rind on)
2 large peaches, peeled and cut into 1/2-inch slices
2 nectarines, cut into 1/2-inch slices

2 plums, cut into 1/4-inch slices
1 cup sweet cherries, pitted
1/2 cup blueberries
1 tablespoon fresh lemon juice
Fresh mint leaves, for garnish (optional)

In a small saucepan, bring the water, sugar and mint to a boil, cover and remove from the heat. Allow to steep for 30 minutes. (This sugar syrup may be made 2 days in advance and refrigerated. Strain out the mint before storing.)

Cut the watermelon from the rind and remove the seeds. Cut in half and purée one piece in a blender or food processor. Cut the other piece into 1-inch chunks and place in a medium-sized bowl. Toss the peaches, nectarines, plums, cherries and blueberries with the watermelon chunks. Add 1/4 cup of the sugar syrup and the lemon juice to the watermelon purée and pour over the fruit mixture. Cover and refrigerate for 1 hour. Stir gently to coat fruit with syrup and garnish with fresh mint, if desired, before serving. *Serves 4*

Nectarines and Prosciutto with Raspberry Vinaigrette

*Choose the most perfect and ripest nectarines from the local
farmers' market to showcase in this salad. Not only will they be more flavorful
than supermarket fruit, but you may also find a variety with intensely red skin or flesh
that would look particularly handsome on the plate.*

2 Belgian endives, halved lengthwise
1/2 pound thinly sliced prosciutto
   (approximately 8 slices)
4 medium nectarines, pitted and sliced into eighths
2 tablespoons finely chopped fresh chives
1 tablespoon finely chopped fresh
   lemon thyme (optional)

Raspberry Vinaigrette:
3 tablespoons raspberry vinegar
1 tablespoon fresh lemon juice
1 tablespoon honey
1/3 cup olive oil
1/3 cup safflower oil
1/8 teaspoon salt
1/4 teaspoon fresh, coarsely ground black pepper

Separate the endive leaves and arrange them in a spoke pattern on 4 salad plates, leaving a circle in the center of each plate. Drape 2 slices of prosciutto in the center spaces of each plate, covering the ends of the endive. Place the nectarine slices between the endive leaves and sprinkle the salads with the chives and thyme.

In a small bowl, whisk together the vinegar, lemon juice, honey, oils, salt and pepper. Drizzle the vinaigrette over the salads and serve immediately. *Serves 4*

Arugula and Sweet Onion Salad with Nectarine Vinaigrette

I am always looking for new ways to enjoy arugula. Here, its peppery bite is balanced by sweet fruit and unctuous cheese. To make this a substantial luncheon entree, add more greens and summer fruit.

Nectarine Vinaigrette:
2 ripe nectarines
2/3 cup safflower oil
4 tablespoons fresh lime juice
3 tablespoons granulated sugar
1/4 teaspoon salt
1/4 teaspoon fresh, coarsely ground black pepper

4 cups loosely packed arugula leaves,
*   washed and dried*
2 large, unpeeled nectarines, cut into 1/2-inch slices
1/2 large sweet onion, such as Vidalia, Maui or
*   Walla Walla*
4 ounces Gorgonzola
Freshly ground black pepper

Pit the nectarines and purée them, unpeeled, in a food processor fitted with a metal blade or in a blender. Add the oil, lime juice, sugar, salt and pepper and pulse until combined. Set aside.

In a large bowl, toss the arugula with approximately three-quarters of the vinaigrette and arrange on 4 salad plates. Lay the nectarine slices on the arugula. Slice the onion into thin rings and divide them among the plates. Crumble the Gorgonzola over the top and drizzle with the remaining vinaigrette. Sprinkle with pepper. *Serves 4*

Plum and Ginger Salad

The intense colors and clean, distinctive tastes make this an assertive first-course salad. To add more drama to the plate, arrange the fruit segments artistically.

6 or 7 ripe red- or black-skinned plums
*   (approximately 1 pound)*
2 navel oranges
2 tablespoons minced fresh ginger
1/2 cup sake or white wine
1/4 cup rice wine vinegar
1 tablespoon soy sauce
1 teaspoon granulated sugar
1/2 cup safflower oil
1 cup mung bean sprouts
1/2 head romaine lettuce, cut into 1/2-inch strips

Cut the plums into 1/2-inch slices. Peel the oranges and separate them into segments.

In a medium bowl, whisk together the ginger, sake, vinegar, soy sauce, sugar and oil. Add the plum and orange slices, toss and marinate for 30 minutes.

Combine the bean sprouts and lettuce and arrange on 6 salad plates. Divide the plums and oranges among the plates and drizzle with the vinaigrette. *Serves 6*

Fruit Salsa with Spicy Pita Chips

This refreshing, complex-tasting hors d'oeuvre is perfect for a hot summer night. Make the salsa a few hours before serving and refrigerate it so that the fruit is chilled and the flavors have time to blend. Although you can make the salsa in a food processor, chopping the fruits by hand gives a prettier texture.

Fruit Salsa:
1 large nectarine
1/2 red or green apple
2 dark-skinned figs
1 orange
1 tablespoon fresh lime juice
1 tablespoon coarsely chopped fresh mint
1 tablespoon coarsely chopped fresh basil
2 tablespoons finely chopped sweet onion, such as
*   Vidalia, Maui or Walla Walla*

Spicy Pita Chips:
3 six-inch pita breads
2 tablespoons safflower oil
1/4 teaspoon cayenne pepper
1/2 teaspoon cumin
1/2 teaspoon ground coriander
1/4 teaspoon salt
1/8 teaspoon fresh, coarsely ground black pepper

Cut the unpeeled nectarine, apple and figs into 1/4-inch dice and place in a medium-sized bowl. Peel the orange, and holding the segments over the bowl to catch the juice, cut them into 1/2-inch pieces. Stir the fruit to combine and add the lime juice, mint, basil and onion. Cover and refrigerate for at least 1 hour. *Makes 1 1/2 cups of salsa*

Preheat the oven to 350 degrees F.

Separate each pita bread into 2 circles. Cut each circle into sixths and brush the surfaces with oil. In a small bowl, combine the spices. Sprinkle the spices over the pita pieces and place on a baking sheet. Bake for 15 minutes, or until lightly browned and crisp. Remove and cool to room temperature. Serve with fruit salsa. If you are not planning to serve the chips within 1 hour, store in an airtight container. *Serves 6 to 8*

Summer Fruit Filled with Goat Cheese and Walnuts

In Europe fruit and cheese are served for dessert, but the same components lend themselves to a
balanced first course. Choose only the ripest and most flavorful fruit, using nectarines and red-fleshed plums
if you can't find good apricots and peaches. Raspberries can replace the blueberries, if desired.

1/2 cup walnuts
2 tablespoons sesame seeds
6 ounces goat cheese, such as Montrachet or Chabis
1 tablespoon finely chopped lemon zest
1 tablespoon plus 1/4 cup walnut oil
1/4 teaspoon fresh, coarsely ground black pepper

Redleaf lettuce leaves, for lining plates
4 apricots
2 large peaches, peeled
1/2 cup blueberries
2 tablespoons fresh lemon juice

Preheat the oven to 350 degrees F. Spread the walnuts in a single layer on a baking sheet and toast in the oven for 10 minutes. Let cool, then chop coarsely. Set aside 2 tablespoons of the walnuts.

In a small, dry sauté pan, toast the sesame seeds, shaking constantly, until golden brown, approximately 3 to 5 minutes. Remove from the pan and set aside.

In a small bowl, combine the remaining walnuts, the sesame seeds, goat cheese, lemon zest, 1 tablespoon of walnut oil and the pepper. (This cheese mixture can be made 1 day ahead and kept covered in the refrigerator.)

Line 4 salad plates with the lettuce leaves. Halve the apricots and peaches and remove the pits. On each plate, arrange 2 apricot halves and 1 peach half, cut side up. Fill the apricots with a rounded teaspoon of the cheese mixture and the peach halves with a rounded tablespoonful. Sprinkle each salad with some blueberries.

In a small bowl, stir together 1/4 cup of walnut oil and the lemon juice. Drizzle over the salads and sprinkle with the remaining 2 tablespoons of walnuts. *Serves 4*

ACCOMPANIMENTS

By the end of July I am completely overwhelmed by the sheer volume of fruit in the markets. There are just not enough hours or meals in the day to enjoy every perfect peach, nectarine, apricot, plum or cherry. For some reason, I always treat each summer as if it were the last. I cannot bear to *not* use every piece of fruit—especially if it grows in my backyard. Fortunately, there are delicious ways to preserve this summer's fruit that will extend some of their pleasure.

Being a bread lover, I naturally evolved into a lover of jam. And stone fruit are the basis of some of our best-loved preserves. Apricot and Orange Marmalade is thick and velvety smooth with a soft bite of orange zest. No commercial pectin is necessary in Raspberry and Cherry Preserves, a most beautiful red. Homemade fruit-based syrups can be canned and given as holiday gifts or poured warm, without restraint, upon Saturday's pancakes. The Poached Pink Peaches can be paired with sliced cold duck breast on tender spinach or used to encircle a seafood salad. Plum Applesauce is one of those comfort foods that seems to have all but disappeared from most cooks' repertoires, but it is still irresistible to all ages.

Clockwise from back: Whole Preserved Greengage Plums in Brandy Syrup (recipe p. 42), Poached Pink Peaches (recipe p. 45) and Bing Cherries Preserved in Port (recipe p. 45)

Apricot and Orange Marmalade

*Two golden fruits combine successfully in this
thick, sweet-tart marmalade. I like biting into a surprise
chunk of orange in my morning spoonful of jam.*

3 pounds apricots
2 tablespoons finely chopped orange zest
1 cup orange sections
2/3 cup fresh orange juice
2 cups granulated sugar

Pit and quarter the apricots. There should be
approximately 9 cups. In a 12-inch skillet or
sauté pan, combine the apricots, zest, orange
sections, juice and sugar. Allow to stand for 1
hour at room temperature.

Place the pan over moderate heat stirring
occasionally, for 1 1/2 hours, or until mixture
looks glazed and no clear liquid is visible.
Continue cooking, stirring constantly, for another 30 minutes until the marmalade is thick.

Sterilize three 8-ounce canning jars by
washing and rinsing them in the dishwasher
without detergent; keep them warm in a 250-
degree-F. oven. Pour boiling water over the
lids to soften the rubber seals. Ladle the hot jam
into the hot jars, filling to within 1/2 inch of the
top. Wipe the rims and seal with the hot lids
and metal bands. Place the jars on a rack, without touching, in a large, deep pot with water to
cover by 1 inch. Cover and boil for 15 minutes.
Use tongs to remove the jars to a cooling rack
and to cool to room temperature. Check the
seals. The jars are sealed when the center of the
lid is slightly indented and cannot be pressed in
with a fingertip. *Makes three 8-ounce jars*

Raspberry and Cherry Preserves

*The raspberries in the preserves retain their
seedy crunch and tartness, while the cherries impart
smoothness and keep their shape.*

2 pounds Bing cherries
8 cups raspberries
3 1/2 cups granulated sugar
2 tablespoons fresh lemon juice

Stem and pit the cherries; you should have 4
cups. In a large bowl, stir together the cherries,
raspberries and sugar. Let stand at room temperature, stirring occasionally, for 2 hours.

Pour the fruit into a wide, shallow,
nonreactive saucepan and stir in the lemon
juice. Cook over moderate heat, stirring occasionally, for 30 to 40 minutes until the mixture
looks thickened and glazed. Remove a tablespoon of the preserves to a small saucer and chill
in the freezer for 5 minutes. Run your finger
through the mixture; if it wrinkles, it is ready to
jar. If it is not ready, continue cooking for 5
more minutes and repeat the test.

Sterilize four 8-ounce canning jars by
washing and rinsing them in the dishwasher
without detergent; keep them warm in a 250-
degree-F. oven. Pour boiling water over the jar
lids to soften the rubber seals. Ladle the hot
preserves to within 1/2 inch of the rims of the
jars. Wipe the rims and seal with the hot lids
and metal bands. Let cool to room temperature, then refrigerate for several weeks. Or,
to store longer, process in a water bath (see
Apricot and Orange Marmalade recipe for
instructions). *Makes four 8-ounce jars*

Whole Preserved Greengage Plums in Brandy Syrup

*Having a pantry filled with homemade preserves gives any cook a sense of security.
These whole plums can be warmed and served with roasted poultry or chilled and lavished with
sabayon for an elegant dessert. Since there is no need to pit or peel the fruit, the recipe is easy
to prepare. Light-skinned Wickson plums can be substituted for the Greengage.*

2 cups granulated sugar
2 cups water
1 tablespoon lemon zest
1 tablespoon fresh lemon juice

1/2 cup Cognac or other brandy
2 1/2 pounds Greengage plums (approximately
    15), left whole
1 high-quality, moist, supple vanilla bean (available
    at specialty markets)

Sterilize two wide-mouthed 1-quart canning jars by washing and rinsing them in the dishwasher without detergent; keep them warm in a 250-degree-F. oven. Pour boiling water over the lids to soften the rubber seals; cover with a towel to keep warm.

In a medium-sized saucepan over high heat, bring the sugar and water to a boil. Add the zest, juice and Cognac and boil for 5 minutes. Add the plums and lower the heat. Simmer for 5 minutes, or until the plums just soften slightly and the skins look glazed.

With a slotted spoon, remove the plums from the syrup and divide between the hot jars. The plums should fit in tightly, but not be crushed. Bring the liquid in the pan to a boil and pour over the fruit, filling the jars to within 1/2 inch of the rim.

Slit the vanilla bean lengthwise, then halve it. Insert one half in each jar.

Wipe the rims carefully and seal with the hot lids and metal bands. Place the jars on a rack, without touching, in a large, deep pot with water to cover by one inch. Cover and boil for 20 minutes. Use tongs to remove the jars to a cooling rack and allow to cool to room temperature and then check the seals. The jars are sealed when the center of the lid is slightly indented and cannot be pressed in with a fingertip. Allow to season for at least 2 weeks before serving. *Makes two 1-quart jars*

Bing Cherries Preserved in Port

Bing Cherries Preserved in Port

Preserved Bing cherries make a wonderful sauce for roast duck or a warm topping for ice cream.

2 cups port
2 cups granulated sugar
1 tablespoon lemon zest in long shreds
1 tablespoon fresh lemon juice
1/4 teaspoon fresh, coarsely ground black pepper
1 pound Bing or other dark sweet cherries, unpitted

Sterilize two 1-pint canning jars by washing and rinsing them in the dishwasher without detergent; keep warm in a 250-degree-F. oven.

In a medium saucepan, combine the port, sugar, zest, lemon juice and pepper. Over medium-high heat, bring the mixture to a boil and cook for 15 minutes, or until reduced by half. Reduce heat to low and stir in the cherries. Cook, stirring constantly, for 10 minutes, or until the cherries are slightly softened.

Pour boiling water over the jar lids to soften the rubber seals. With a slotted spoon, remove the cherries from the syrup and divide between the 2 jars. Bring the syrup to a boil and pour over the cherries to within 1/2 inch of the rims of the jars. Wipe the rims and seal with the hot lids and metal bands. Let cool to room temperature, then refrigerate for several weeks. Or, to store longer, process in a water bath (see Apricot and Orange Marmalade recipe on page 41 for instructions). *Makes two 1-pint jars*

Poached Pink Peaches

Although yellow-fleshed peaches can be used in this taste-tingling dessert, white peaches look beautiful when lightly tinged with the pink wine syrup. Serve this dish as an accompaniment to a summer luncheon salad of roast duck breast or cold herbed chicken, or with brandy snaps as a light dessert.

4 white, slightly firm peaches
1 bottle (750 ml) white Zinfandel
1/3 cup granulated sugar
5 whole cloves
2 teaspoons aniseed
4 sprigs fresh mint, for garnish
1 cup raspberries (optional)

Bring a large saucepan of water to a boil and immerse the peaches for 1 minute. Remove them with a slotted spoon and slip off their skins. Set them aside.

In a medium-sized saucepan large enough to hold the peaches, combine the wine, sugar, cloves and aniseed and cook over high heat for 5 minutes. Add the peaches, reduce the heat to low and cook for 10 minutes. Remove the peaches to a bowl. Bring the wine back to a boil and cook over high heat for approximately 20 minutes until the liquid is reduced to 1 cup. Strain the liquid over the peaches, cover and refrigerate at least 1 hour or overnight.

To serve, place the peaches in a shallow glass dish, pour the syrup over the top and garnish with the mint and raspberries. *Serves 4*

Whole Wheat Peach Muffins

*In this moist, golden muffin, puréed peaches replace some of the oil and liquids, and chunks of peach
intensify the fruity flavor. For a sweeter taste, sprinkle the tops with a little granulated sugar.*

4 peaches (approximately 1 3/4 pounds)
1 cup whole wheat flour, preferably stone-ground
1 1/2 cups all-purpose flour
1 tablespoon baking powder
1/2 teaspoon baking soda
2/3 cup firmly packed dark brown sugar

1/2 teaspoon ground cinnamon
1 teaspoon ground ginger
1/4 teaspoon salt
1/4 cup safflower oil
1 large egg
4 teaspoons granulated sugar (optional)

Preheat the oven to 400 degrees F.

Peel 3 of the peaches, pit and cut into chunks. Purée them in a food processor or blender. You should have 1 1/2 cups. Cut the remaining peach, unpeeled, into 1/2-inch pieces and set aside.

In a large mixing bowl, combine the flours, baking powder and soda, sugar, cinnamon, ginger and salt. Make a well in the center and pour in the peach purée, the oil and the egg. Stir the dry ingredients with the wet just until moistened and then fold in the chopped peaches.

Grease 8 large muffin cups (or use paper liners). Fill the muffin cups with the batter to the top, mounding the batter slightly. Sprinkle the sugar over the batter, if desired, before baking. Bake in the center of the oven for 25 to 30 minutes, or until a toothpick inserted in the center comes out clean and the tops are cracked. Remove from the pan and cool completely. *Makes 8 large muffins*

Cherry Pecan Coffee Cake

Weekend mornings deserve special breakfasts, and this fragrant quick bread makes them so. To save yourself time in the morning, prepare the topping the night before.

Topping:
3/4 cup pecan halves
4 tablespoons unsalted butter, melted
1/2 cup all-purpose flour
2/3 cup firmly packed dark brown sugar
1/2 teaspoon cinnamon
3/4 pound dark sweet cherries, pitted (approximately 2 cups)

8 tablespoons unsalted butter
1/2 cup granulated sugar
1 large egg
1/2 cup plain low-fat yogurt
1 1/2 teaspoons pure vanilla extract
1 1/2 cups all-purpose flour
2 teaspoons baking powder
1/2 teaspoon baking soda
1/2 teaspoon salt

Preheat the oven to 350 degrees F.

Spread the pecans on a baking sheet and bake for 15 minutes, or until lightly toasted.

In a medium-sized bowl, stir together the pecans and the remaining topping ingredients. Set aside.

In a large mixing bowl, cream the butter and sugar until smooth. Beat in the egg, yogurt and vanilla until well combined. In a small bowl, stir together the flour, baking powder and soda, and salt and add to the butter mixture, stirring just until incorporated. The batter will be stiff and very sticky.

Raise the heat to 375 degrees F. Butter a 9-inch quiche dish or square baking pan and spread the batter evenly over the bottom. Crumble the cherry topping over the batter and bake in the center of the oven for 35 to 40 minutes until golden brown and the center does not jiggle when lightly shaken. Remove from the oven and cool on a rack. *Serves 6 to 8*

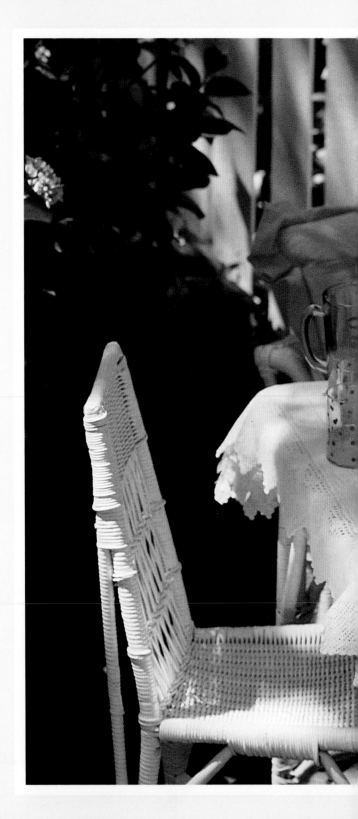

Cranberry and Nectarine Jam

This is an example of a cross-season jam: Cranberries and nectarines are not in the market at the same time. If you forgot to toss a couple of bags of cranberries into the freezer last fall, most stores now stock them frozen year-round. Frozen cranberries add natural pectin, tartness and vibrant color to the nectarines.

5 large nectarines (approximately 1 pound)
2 cups granulated sugar

3 cups fresh or frozen cranberries
*   (approximately 3/4 pound)*
1 tablespoon fresh lemon juice

Cut the unpeeled nectarines into 1-inch chunks. Toss them in a large bowl with 1 cup of sugar. Set aside for 2 hours at room temperature.

Sterilize four 8-ounce canning jars by washing and rinsing them in the dishwasher without detergent; keep them warm in a 250-degree-F. oven.

In a large saucepan, stir together the cranberries and remaining 1 cup of sugar. Place over moderate heat and cook, stirring constantly, approximately 10 minutes, or until the cranberries pop. Stir in the nectarines and all of their juices. Add the lemon juice. Continue cooking over moderate heat, stirring occasionally, for 20 minutes, or until the mixture thickens.

Pour boiling water over the jar lids to soften the rubber seals. Ladle the hot jam into the jars, filling to within 1/2 inch of the top. Wipe the rims carefully and seal with the hot lids and metal bands. Place the jars on a rack, without touching, in a large, deep pot with water to cover by one inch. Cover and boil for 15 minutes. Use tongs to remove the jars to a cooling rack and allow to cool to room temperature and then check the seals. The jars are sealed when the center of the lid is slightly indented and cannot be pressed in with a fingertip. *Makes four 8-ounce jars*

Plum Applesauce

*In early fall, when you can still find plums in the markets,
don't completely succumb to the tantalizing abundance of apples and pears—stir a little
summer color and taste into a wonderful homemade applesauce. The plummy
result is perfect for fickle weather. Pair it with barbecued ribs on a suddenly chilly night, or
spoon it over pillowy pancakes for a breakfast outside on a balmy Saturday.*

2 1/2 pounds dark-skinned plums (approximately 15)
3 1/2 pounds flavorful green or red apples, such as
*   Granny Smith, Golden or Red Delicious or*
*   Gravenstein*

2 cups unsweetened apple juice
1 cup granulated sugar
1/4 teaspoon ground cinnamon
1/8 teaspoon ground cloves
2 teaspoons fresh lemon juice

Quarter the plums and discard the pits. Quarter the apples and combine with the plums and apple juice in a large pot. Over high heat, bring the mixture to a boil, cover, and then reduce heat to moderate. Cook for 30 minutes, or until the fruit can be mashed with the back of a spoon. Put the fruit and the liquid through a food mill, ricer or a large-meshed strainer. Discard the peels and residue. There should be approximately 7 cups of sauce. At this point the mixture can be covered and refrigerated for up to 2 days.

Pour the sauce into a large sauté pan and place over moderate heat. Stir in the sugar, cinnamon, cloves and lemon juice. Continue cooking for approximately 45 minutes, or until the sauce is thickened and has reduced to 5 cups. Let cool to room temperature and refrigerate. Taste and adjust seasonings or sugar if necessary. *Makes 5 cups*

MAIN COURSES

Our summer stone fruits can merge and mingle with foods from all parts of the world. Asian-influenced dishes work particularly well with fruit, but the flavors of Middle Eastern and Mediterranean cooking are also very compatible. I like the smoothness of yellow peaches in the Peach and Ginger Chicken Stir-fry. A hearty, multitextured rice salad gains color and complexity with the addition of apricots, peaches and plums. Moroccan Lamb and Fruit Stew derives its balance from the way the slightly tart apricots and nectarines offset the lamb chunks.

Summer fruit can also be cooked down to a thick, naturally sweet sauce that eliminates the need for cream or other thickeners. Sautéed Shrimp with Spicy Apricot Ginger Sauce deserves a place in your summer dinner menus: Its golden, peppery sauce says summer to your eye as it zaps your palate. Basting and broiling fruit halves caramelizes their edges without impairing their firmness. Use them to surround a mound of quickly prepared couscous for a vegetarian main course that will please the cook with its ease and diners with its flavor.

Experiment with other familiar main courses by adding sliced, unpeeled peaches, apricots, nectarines and plums to them—you'll add a lovely summer touch.

Chicken, Avocado, Orange and Nectarine Salad
with Citrus Yogurt Dressing

At some point during the summer, I always crave a chicken salad. Although chicken salad has been served inside nearly every imaginable fruit, I feel that incorporating the nectarines and oranges into the salad gives the chicken extra moisture and zest. This dressing is very low in fat for more summer lightness.

Citrus Yogurt Dressing:
1/2 cup plain low-fat or whole-milk yogurt
1/4 cup fresh orange juice
3 tablespoons safflower oil
1 tablespoon fresh lemon juice
2 tablespoons poppy seeds
2 teaspoons granulated sugar
2 teaspoons grated lemon zest
1/2 teaspoon salt

1 roasted chicken, weighing approximately
  3 pounds
1 avocado
4 medium nectarines
2 navel oranges
Arugula leaves, for lining plates
2 tablespoons finely chopped Italian parsley,
  for garnish

In a small bowl, whisk together the yogurt, orange juice, oil, lemon juice, poppy seeds, sugar, zest and salt. Allow to stand at room temperature for 1 hour.

Remove the skin from the chicken and discard. Pull the meat from the bones and cut into 1-inch pieces. There should be approximately 4 cups. Place in a large bowl. Peel the avocado, cut it into 1/2-inch slices and add to the chicken. Cut the unpeeled nectarines into 1-inch chunks and add to the salad. Peel the oranges, divide into sections and toss with the other ingredients. Pour the dressing on top and mix well.

Line 4 plates with arugula leaves and divide the salad among them. Garnish with the parsley and serve. *Serves 4*

Fruited Rice Salad with Toasted Pine Nuts

You can, of course, make this salad with only one kind of rice,
but I find the mixture of textures and flavors more interesting. My mother always said she didn't like cold rice.
But this delicious dish is not what she had in mind.

1/4 cup wild rice
1/4 teaspoon salt
1/2 cup brown rice
1/4 cup currants or dried cherries (or a combination)
1 1/2 cups vegetable or chicken stock
3 cups basmati rice
1/4 teaspoon salt
1/2 cup pine nuts
1/4 cup diced red bell pepper
1/4 cup finely chopped celery
1/3 cup finely chopped Italian parsley

4 nectarines, unpeeled and cut into 1/2-inch cubes
2 peaches, peeled and cut into 1/2-inch cubes
2 plums, unpeeled and cut into 1/2-inch slices

Vinaigrette:
4 tablespoons sherry or white wine vinegar
2 tablespoons orange juice
2 tablespoons Dijon mustard
1 tablespoon honey
1 1/3 cups safflower oil
1/4 teaspoon salt
1/4 teaspoon coarsely ground black pepper

Pour the wild rice into a pot with 1 1/2 cups cold water. Add 1/4 teaspoon of salt and bring to a boil. Cover, reduce heat to a simmer and cook for 1 hour, or until all grains are tender. Drain and let cool. Meanwhile, pour the brown rice and the currants into a pot of the boiling vegetable or chicken stock. Cover, lower the heat to a simmer and cook for 50 minutes, or until the rice is tender. Cool to room temperature.

Stir the basmati rice into a pot with 1 3/4 cups boiling water. Add 1/4 teaspoon of salt, cover and cook on low heat for 15 minutes. Remove from the heat, fluff rice with a fork and set aside to cool. There should be a total of 5 cups of rice.

In a small, dry sauté pan, toast the pine nuts, shaking constantly, until golden brown, approximately for 3 to 5 minutes. Remove from the pan and set aside.

In a large bowl, combine the rice, bell pepper, celery, parsley, nectarines, peaches and plums.

In a small bowl, whisk together the ingredients for the vinaigrette and pour over the rice mixture. Toss well, sprinkle with the pine nuts and serve immediately.

If desired, the salad can be refrigerated overnight, covered, without the pine nuts. Bring to room temperature and add the pine nuts before serving. *Serves 6 as a main dish, 8 as a salad*

Peach and Ginger Chicken Stir-fry

*Peaches and ginger are natural partners. Combine them with strips of
boneless chicken and Asian seasonings for a quick meal made in a wok or skillet. For variety,
toss in a cup of frozen green peas in the last three minutes of cooking.*

4 boneless, skinless chicken breast halves
    (approximately 1 1/2 pounds)
1 egg white
1 tablespoon cornstarch
1/4 teaspoon salt
2 tablespoons mirin (Japanese sweet rice wine) or sherry
1 tablespoon rice wine vinegar
1 tablespoon soy sauce

2 tablespoons vegetable oil
2 tablespoons minced fresh ginger
3 cloves garlic, minced
3 unpeeled ripe peaches, cut into sixths
1 tablespoon finely chopped fresh mint
2 tablespoons finely chopped fresh cilantro
2 tablespoons finely chopped roasted cashews (optional)
Steamed rice, for accompaniment

Cut the chicken into 1/2-inch strips. In a medium-sized bowl, toss the chicken with the egg white, cornstarch and salt. Set aside.

In a small bowl, stir together the mirin, vinegar and soy sauce.

Heat the oil in a wok or heavy skillet, and over moderate heat, sauté the ginger and garlic until fragrant. Turn the heat to high, add the chicken and cook quickly until opaque. Add the peaches, stirring and scraping the bottom of the wok constantly, and sauté until lightly browned. Add the mirin mixture and cook approximately 2 minutes until the ingredients are well coated and the liquid has thickened. Sprinkle with the mint, cilantro and cashews, if using, and serve with steamed rice. *Serves 4*

Oven-Roasted Summer Fruit on Couscous

Couscous is a grain which takes less than 10 minutes to prepare. Paired with roasted fruits basted with an Asian-flavored sauce, it makes a fine vegetarian entree for a warm summer night. Lightly steamed snow peas and water chestnuts would make a fine accompaniment.

1/4 cup sesame seeds
2 tablespoons soy sauce
4 tablespoons honey
1 tablespoon firmly packed light or dark brown sugar
2 tablespoons safflower oil
1 tablespoon rice wine vinegar
2 tablespoons minced fresh ginger
2 cloves garlic, minced
2 nectarines
1 peach
3 plums

4 apricots
4 firm figs

Couscous:
One 14 1/2-ounce can chicken or vegetable broth
3 tablespoons rice wine vinegar
Water, as needed
1/4 teaspoon salt
2 tablespoons unsalted butter
1 tablespoon currants
1 1/2 cups couscous

1/4 cup finely chopped Italian parsley

In a small, dry sauté pan, toast the sesame seeds, shaking constantly, until golden brown, approximately for 3 to 5 minutes. Remove from the pan and set aside.

In a small bowl, stir together the soy sauce, honey, brown sugar, oil, vinegar, ginger and garlic.

Preheat the broiler and place a rack directly under the heat source. Place a roasting rack on a rimmed baking sheet lined with foil.

Quarter and pit the nectarines and the peach. Pit the plums and halve them, or if they are large, quarter them. Halve and pit the apricots and halve the figs. Dip the fruit pieces into the basting sauce and lay them cut side up on the roasting rack.

Broil for 3 minutes, brush with sauce, then broil 3 to 4 minutes more until the fruit is just singed and lightly glazed. Remove from the oven and cover with foil to keep warm.

Pour the broth and vinegar into a 1-quart measuring cup. Add water until you have 2 1/4 cups liquid. Pour into a medium-sized saucepan and add the salt, butter and currants. Bring to a boil and stir in the couscous. Cover the pan and remove from the heat. Allow the couscous to stand for 5 to 7 minutes, then fluff with a fork.

To serve, mound the couscous in the center of a large platter and surround it with the fruit. Drizzle with the remaining basting sauce and garnish with the sesame seeds and parsley.
Serves 4 or 5

Roast Pork Tenderloin with Peach Mustard Crust

Pork tenderloin is both economical and low in fat. The fruity mustard crust
ensures that the meat will remain moist and flavorful during roasting. Thin slices of the pork
on rye bread spread with more of the mustard make perfect picnic fare.

1/2 cup fresh bread crumbs
1 teaspoon salt
1/2 teaspoon fresh, coarsely ground black pepper

2 tablespoons olive oil
1 cup Peaches and Honey Mustard (see recipe opposite)
1 1/2 to 2 pounds boneless pork tenderloin

In a small bowl, combine the bread crumbs, salt, pepper, olive oil and 1/2 cup of Peaches and Honey Mustard. Pat the mixture on the meat, wrap tightly in plastic wrap and refrigerate overnight, or let stand for several hours at room temperature.

When ready to cook, bring the pork to room temperature and preheat the oven to 400 degrees F.

Place the pork in a shallow roasting pan and bake in the center of the oven for 40 to 45 minutes, or until the internal temperature registers 155 degrees F. Slice into 1/2-inch pieces and serve. Or cool to room temperature before slicing and serving. Accompany with the remaining Peaches and Honey Mustard. *Serves 4 or 5*

Peaches and Honey Mustard

*I was looking for an ingredient to temper the fire of powdered mustard and thought about
mellow, sweet peaches. Not only do they provide a good balance, they also help thicken the sauce naturally.
This intense sweet-hot mustard is perfect for spreading on rye bread for ham sandwiches, slathering
on skinless chicken breasts before grilling, or whisking into a basic vinaigrette.*

3 very ripe yellow peaches
2 tablespoons yellow mustard seed
1 cup white wine vinegar
1/2 cup apple juice
1/4 cup honey

1/2 cup loosely packed light brown sugar
1 clove garlic, minced
1/2 teaspoon ground ginger
1/2 cup powdered mustard
1 1/2 teaspoons salt

Peel the peaches and cut them into 1-inch cubes. Grind the mustard seed briefly in a spice grinder until cracked but not powdered.

In a 9- or 10-inch nonreactive skillet, stir together the peaches, mustard seed, vinegar, apple juice, honey, brown sugar, garlic, ginger, powdered mustard and salt. Cover and cook over low heat, stirring occasionally to prevent sticking, for approximately 1 hour, or until the peaches are very soft and the liquid is the thickness of sour cream. Remove from the heat and purée in a food processor or blender. Let cool. If not using immediately, pour into a clean, dry jar or bowl, cover tightly and refrigerate for up to 3 weeks.

If you wish to store the mustard longer than 3 weeks, sterilize 2 half-pint canning jars by washing and rinsing them in the dishwasher without detergent; keep them warm in a 250-degree-F. oven.

Pour boiling water over the jar lids to soften the rubber seals; cover with a towel to keep warm. Pour the sauce into the hot jars. Wipe the rims carefully and seal with the hot lids and metal bands. Place the jars on a rack, without touching, in a large, deep pot with water to cover by one inch. Cover and boil for 15 minutes. Use tongs to remove the jars to a cooling rack and allow to cool to room temperature and then check the seals. The jars are sealed when the center of the lid is slightly indented and cannot be pressed in with a fingertip. Store at room temperature. *Makes 2 cups*

Moroccan Lamb and Fruit Stew

Lighter than the traditional lamb stew with thickened juices, this version is perfect for summer.
By stirring in the fruits after the lamb has simmered to tenderness, you will preserve their colors and shapes.

2 pounds boneless lamb, trimmed of all fat and cut
    into 2-by-inch pieces
1/4 teaspoon cayenne pepper
1 teaspoon salt
1 tablespoon minced fresh ginger
1 cup plain low-fat yogurt
2 tablespoons olive oil
1/4 teaspoon fresh, coarsely ground black pepper

1/2 teaspoon turmeric
1/4 teaspoon cinnamon
1/4 teaspoon ground coriander
1/2 cup water
5 apricots, pitted and quartered
2 nectarines, pitted and cut into 1/4-inch slices
1/2 cup finely chopped fresh cilantro
Steamed brown rice, for accompaniment

In a large, shallow bowl, toss the lamb with the cayenne and salt. Stir the ginger into the yogurt and pour over the lamb. Turn the lamb pieces to coat them well on all sides. Cover the bowl and marinate for 1 hour at room temperature or several hours in the refrigerator.

Heat the olive oil in a heavy 10- or 12-inch skillet over high heat. Sprinkle in the black pepper, turmeric, cinnamon and coriander. Stir for 1 minute until the spices are very fragrant and sizzling. Add the lamb and all the marinade and stir well. The mixture will turn bright yellow because of the turmeric.

Bring to a boil, cover and reduce heat to low. Cook undisturbed for 1 hour, then gently add the 1/2 cup of water. Cover again and cook for 15 minutes. Remove the cover and continue cooking for another 15 minutes. Stir in the apricots and nectarines. Cook, stirring gently, for 5 to 6 minutes until the fruit has softened slightly. Sprinkle with the cilantro and serve over brown rice. *Serves 4*

Sautéed Shrimp with Spicy Apricot Ginger Sauce

Bright, fruity Asian flavors make this fast summer dinner appealing. If you can't find the chili paste with garlic in the Asian section of the supermarket, substitute 1/2 teaspoon red pepper flakes.

1 pound large shrimp (24 to 28 shrimp)
2 teaspoons cornstarch
2 tablespoons olive oil
1/2 teaspoon coarse salt
1/4 teaspoon fresh, coarsely ground black pepper

Spicy Apricot Ginger Sauce:
1 pound apricots
4 cloves garlic, minced
3 tablespoons minced fresh ginger

2 tablespoons olive oil
1/2 cup fresh lime or lemon juice
2 tablespoons sherry or sherry wine vinegar
3 tablespoons brown sugar
1/2 teaspoon chili paste with garlic
1/4 teaspoon salt

1/3 cup finely chopped fresh cilantro
Steamed white rice, for accompaniment

Peel and devein the shrimp. In a medium-sized bowl, toss the shrimp with the cornstarch, olive oil, salt and pepper. Set aside.

Pit the apricots and purée them in a food processor. Set aside.

In a medium saucepan over moderate heat sauté the garlic and ginger in the olive oil until fragrant. Add the apricot purée, the lime juice, sherry, brown sugar, chili paste and salt. Cook, stirring occasionally, for 20 minutes. (The sauce can be prepared up to 2 days ahead and kept covered and refrigerated.)

In a 9- or 10-inch skillet or wok over high heat, sauté the shrimp until they change color. Pour in 1 1/2 cups of the Spicy Apricot Ginger Sauce and continue tossing and cooking until the shrimp are well coated with thickened sauce. Garnish with the cilantro and serve over steamed rice. Pass the remaining sauce. *Serves 4*

SWEETS

Frankly, when I think of summer fruit I think first of desserts: bubbly, homely cobblers; *clafouti* with golden apricots peeking out of the custard; lattice-topped pies, crusts stained with baked-on fruit juices; ice creams that team puréed fruit with cream; sorbets that call for little more than fruit and sugar.

For some folks, just a fragrant nectarine, several nugget-like apricots, or a fistful of skin-staining cherries is quite enough after a meal. But I love the artistry these fruits can elicit. Smooth, shiny yellow arcs of peaches with red-kissed centers are stunning next to thimble-sized raspberries, all atop a frangipane filling. Sometimes cooked, but often simply arranged on a pastry, stone fruits can be turned into a dessert as traditional as Vermont Maple Syrup and Peach Pie or as innovative as Tempura Peaches with Lemon Sabayon.

In almost every recipe that calls for peaches, you can substitute nectarines, and sometimes apricots. Cooking with plums requires more attention to sugar since there is much more variation among plum varieties. Remember that the end product is only as wonderful as the ingredients, so select the ripest, most aromatic fruit you can find.

Left to right: Crustless Ricotta Cheesecake Topped with Nectarines and Raspberries (recipe p. 68), Apricots in a Puff Pastry Shell (recipe p. 72) and Frangipane Tart with Summer Fruit (recipe p. 71)

Crustless Ricotta Cheesecake Topped with Nectarines and Raspberries

This is the perfect summer dessert: Slightly sweet and airy cheeses topped with the ripest fruit available. For the best flavor and texture, remove the cheesecake from the refrigerator at least one hour before serving. It's also delicious still warm, just a few hours out of the oven. You can substitute peaches for the nectarines, or use all Bing cherries.

1 tablespoon unsalted butter, softened
All-purpose flour, for dusting
3 cups (1 1/2 pounds) whole-milk ricotta cheese
5 ounces goat cheese, such as Montrachet
4 large eggs, separated
1 large egg yolk
3/4 cup granulated sugar
1 teaspoon pure vanilla extract

1 tablespoon finely chopped lemon zest
3 tablespoons all-purpose flour
2 ripe nectarines
1 cup raspberries
Confectioners' sugar, for dusting (optional)
Melted apple jelly, for brushing fruit (optional)
Raspberry Sauce (see opposite page, optional)

Preheat the oven to 300 degrees F.

Coat the bottom and sides of an 8 1/2-inch springform pan with the butter. Sprinkle with flour and tap out any excess.

In a food processor fitted with the metal blade, process the ricotta and goat cheese until combined. Add the 5 egg yolks, 1/4 cup of the sugar, the vanilla, zest and flour. Process until completely smooth.

In a large mixing bowl, beat the egg whites on high speed until foamy. Gradually add the remaining 1/2 cup of sugar and continue beating until the whites are thick and creamy and look like marshmallow cream. Fold 1/3 of the whites into the cheese mixture, then add the cheese mixture to the remaining whites.

Continue folding until no more whites are visible. Pour into the prepared pan, smooth the top and place in the center of the oven. Bake for 1 hour and 30 minutes until the cheesecake has risen to the top of the pan and is very pale. Remove and let cool to room temperature. Cover and refrigerate overnight.

To serve, cut the unpeeled nectarines into 1/4-inch slices and arrange in concentric circles, barely overlapping, over the top of the cake, leaving a 3-inch space in the center. Fill the space with raspberries. Dust the fruit heavily with confectioners' sugar or brush with melted apple jelly, if desired. Alternatively, drizzle individual slices with Raspberry Sauce. *Serves 8 to 10*

Raspberry Sauce

Intensely red and full of raspberry flavor, this is a convenient sauce to dress up many desserts.

Two 10-ounce tins frozen raspberries in sugar
    syrup,* thawed
1/4 cup granulated sugar

1 tablespoon fresh lemon juice
2 teaspoons cornstarch
2 tablespoons framboise, crème de cassis or kirsch

Using the back of a spoon, press the raspberries through a sieve into a small saucepan. Scrape the bottom of the sieve to push as much pulp through as possible. Stir in the sugar and the lemon juice. Place over high heat and bring the mixture to a boil.

In a small cup, dissolve the cornstarch in the liqueur and add to the raspberry mixture. Cook for 2 minutes, stirring, until the sauce is just thickened. Let cool to room temperature, then cover and refrigerate until ready to use. *Makes 1 1/2 cups sauce*

*Available in specialty stores

Frangipane Tart with Summer Fruit

Let this wonderful almond-flavored tart become the canvas for an artistic fruit composition. Nectarines and peaches are spectacular surrounding a mound of raspberries. But red-fleshed plums with cool green slices of kiwi, blackberries, pitted Royal Ann cherries, golden apricots and sweet Bing cherries make a lovely variation.

Pastry:
1 1/2 cups all-purpose flour
1/4 cup granulated sugar
8 tablespoons unsalted butter
1 egg yolk
2 to 3 tablespoons milk

Frangipane:
2 cups blanched almonds
1 1/3 cups granulated sugar

4 large eggs
1/4 teaspoon pure almond extract

2 nectarines
2 peaches
3 plums
1/2 cup raspberries or blueberries
1/4 kiwi
Melted apple jelly, for glazing (optional)

To make the pastry, place the flour and sugar in a mixing bowl and stir. Cut the butter into 1/2-inch cubes and add to the flour mixture. With a pastry blender or two knives, cut in until the mixture resembles coarse meal.

In a small bowl, whisk together the egg yolk and milk and pour onto the flour mixture. Stir lightly with a fork to moisten, then gather the dough into a ball with your hands. Press the dough into a flat disk, wrap tightly in plastic wrap and refrigerate for 2 hours.

On a lightly floured surface, roll the dough into a 12-inch circle. Fit into a 10-inch tart pan with a removable bottom. Prick the bottom of the shell lightly with a fork and refrigerate for 30 minutes.

Preheat the oven to 425 degrees F.

Line the shell with wax paper or round coffee filters and fill with pastry weights or rice. Place it on a baking sheet and bake in the lower third of the oven for 15 minutes. Remove the

paper and weights and bake for another 5 to 7 minutes, or until pale golden. Remove the pastry shell and turn the oven down to 375 degrees F.

In a food processor, grind the almonds with 2/3 cup of the sugar until powdery. Add the remaining sugar, the eggs and almond extract and pulse until blended. Carefully pour the frangipane into the partially baked tart shell and bake in the lower third of the oven for 20 to 30 minutes, or until the filling looks puffed and golden. Allow the tart to cool completely in the pan. Remove the sides and transfer the tart to a serving platter.

Cut the unpeeled nectarines, peaches and plums into 1/4-inch slices. Arrange the slices in concentric circles on top of the tart. Place raspberries at intervals in the circles and fill the very center with thinly sliced kiwi. Glaze the fruits with melted apple jelly, if desired. Makes one 10-inch tart. *Serves 10*

Apricots in a Puff Pastry Shell

Many local bakeries sell high-quality puff pastry, usually frozen. What you find in the frozen-food section of the supermarket is made with oil instead of butter and has a less appealing taste.

8 ounces puff pastry, very cold
12 apricots (or substitute 3 nectarines,
*   cut into eighths)*
1/2 cup loosely packed light brown sugar
2 tablespoons all-purpose flour

1 teaspoon pure vanilla extract
1/8 teaspoon freshly grated nutmeg
Granulated sugar, for sprinkling
1 beaten egg, for brushing pastry
Vanilla ice cream, for accompaniment

Preheat the oven to 400 degrees F.

On a lightly floured surface, roll the pastry, while still cold, into a 12-inch square. Place on a baking sheet. Fold the edges in on all sides to form 1/2-inch borders, leaving the corners unfolded. Twist the points of the corners together and press against the baking sheet.

Slice the apricots in half and toss in a bowl with the sugar, flour, vanilla and nutmeg.

Arrange the fruit in five rows across the pastry, keeping within the borders. Sprinkle the fruit lightly with granulated sugar and brush the pastry borders with the beaten egg. Bake in the lower third of the oven for 20 to 25 minutes, or until browned and puffed. Cool for 5 minutes and serve with vanilla ice cream. *Serves 6*

Apricot Clafouti

A clafouti is a French custard and fruit dessert usually made with cherries.
Because clafoutis can be made with ingredients commonly found in most kitchens, all you
need to add is wonderful ripe summer fruit for a delicious creation.

1 pound fresh apricots, sliced 1/4 inch thick
1 cup half-and-half or whole milk
2 large eggs
3 tablespoons Cognac

1/3 cup granulated sugar
1/2 cup less 1 tablespoon all-purpose flour
Freshly grated nutmeg
Sifted confectioners' sugar, for dusting

Preheat the oven to 350 degrees F.

Butter a 1-quart shallow baking or gratin dish and arrange the apricots over the bottom.

In a blender or food processor, combine the half-and-half, eggs, Cognac and sugar. Add the flour and blend until smooth. Pour the mixture over the apricots. Grate the nutmeg over the custard and bake in the center of the oven for 30 to 35 minutes, or until the *clafouti* is golden and puffed. Allow to cool for 5 minutes, sprinkle heavily with confectioners' sugar and serve. *Serves 4 to 5*

Sour Cherry Cobbler

*In Michigan, where sour cherries are abundant, cooks pit them and toss them into
1-pound freezer bags. Baked into a pie or cobbler after the season ends, these tart, distinctive cherries
are almost impossible to distinguish from fresh ones. Here the usual pastry crust is replaced with
a soft, tender buttermilk dough that resembles a light steamed pudding.*

Filling:
4 cups fresh or frozen sour cherries
3/4 cup granulated sugar
1 1/2 tablespoons cornstarch
1 tablespoon fresh lemon juice

Topping:
4 tablespoons unsalted butter, at room temperature
1/3 cup granulated sugar

1 cup all-purpose flour
2 teaspoons baking powder
1/2 teaspoon baking soda
1/4 teaspoon salt
1 teaspoon finely chopped lemon zest
1/2 cup buttermilk

Vanilla or cinnamon ice cream, for accompaniment

In a medium-sized saucepan, off the heat, stir together the cherries and sugar and allow to macerate for 30 minutes. Pour off 1/2 cup of the accumulated juice into a small bowl and dissolve the cornstarch in it. Return the juice to the saucepan, turn the heat to high and bring to a boil. Stir constantly for approximately 2 minutes until the liquid has thickened slightly and the cherries look glazed. Remove from the heat and stir in the lemon juice. Set aside.

Preheat the oven to 375 degrees F.

In a food processor fitted with a metal blade, or using an electric mixer on medium speed, combine the butter and sugar until light and fluffy. Add the flour, baking powder and soda, salt, zest and buttermilk and mix until well combined. The batter will be very sticky.

Pour the cherries into a 9-inch square baking dish or a 7-by-11-inch baking pan. Drop the batter by rounded tablespoonfuls onto the cherries. There will still be filling showing. Place the cobbler in the center of the oven and bake for 40 to 45 minutes until the top is golden brown and the filling is bubbling. Remove and let cool for 15 minutes. Serve warm with ice cream. *Serves 6*

Tempura Peaches with Lemon Sabayon

This dish has a wonderful play of textures: The tenderness of a well-ripened peach is encrusted with lacy tempura batter and surrounded with silky lemon sauce. You can substitute nectarine, apricot or plum halves for the peaches, or make a beautiful fruit medley with all four. Freestone peaches are the easiest to pit.

Lemon Sabayon:
3 tablespoons cornstarch
1/2 cup fresh lemon juice
1 1/2 cups Chardonnay
2 teaspoons finely chopped lemon zest
3 egg yolks
1 cup granulated sugar

Tempura Batter:
1/2 cup cake flour
1/4 cup cornstarch
1/2 teaspoon baking powder
1 large egg white
1 1/4 cups very cold sparkling water or club soda

4 large ripe freestone peaches, unpeeled
Vegetable oil, for deep-frying
Confectioners' sugar, for dusting

In the top of a double boiler, whisk the cornstarch into the lemon juice until dissolved. Whisk in the wine, zest, yolks and sugar and set over simmering water. Continue cooking and whisking for approximately 15 minutes until the mixture comes to a boil, thickens and becomes very smooth. Remove the sauce from the heat, cover to keep warm, and set aside.

In a medium-sized bowl, stir together the flour, cornstarch and baking powder. In a small bowl, beat the egg white and sparkling water with a fork until frothy and add to the dry ingredients. Stir until moistened but still lumpy. If the batter becomes too thin (the lumps will disappear and it won't cling well to the fruits), stir in a little more flour. Set the bowl inside a larger bowl filled with ice cubes. It is important to keep the batter very cold; the crispiness of the tempura comes from immersing cold batter into hot oil.

Halve and pit the peaches. Pat them dry with a paper towel. Dip each half into the batter, then drop into at least 3 inches of oil heated to 375 degrees F. Fry until golden brown, turning once, then transfer with a slotted spoon to paper towels to drain. Place the peaches, cut side down, on a plate and dust with confectioners' sugar. Pass the sabayon. *Serves 8*

Cherry and Ganache Tart in a Spiced Nut Crust

*This cinnamon-scented cookielike crust is spread with rich chocolate
and balanced with sparkling fresh fruit. Instead of the cherries, try thinly sliced
apricots or nectarines or a combination of fruits.*

Spiced Nut Crust:
3/4 cup walnuts
3/4 cup all-purpose flour
1/4 teaspoon salt
1 teaspoon cinnamon
1/2 teaspoon freshly grated nutmeg
1/3 cup firmly packed light brown sugar
4 tablespoons unsalted butter, cold
2 tablespoons ice water

6 ounces semisweet chocolate
1/2 cup heavy cream
1 pound pitted dark sweet whole cherries
  (approximately 3 cups)
Melted currant or apple jelly, for glazing (optional)
Confectioners' sugar, for dusting (optional)

Preheat the oven to 350 degrees F.

In a food processor fitted with the metal blade, grind the walnuts finely. Place on a baking sheet and toast in the oven for 10 minutes. Remove and let cool.

Return to the food processor and add the flour, salt, cinnamon, nutmeg and sugar and pulse to combine. Cut the butter into small pieces and process until the mixture resembles coarse meal. Add the ice water and pulse until the dough holds together when pressed between two fingers. Turn the dough out onto a piece of plastic wrap and press into a disk. Refrigerate it, wrapped in the plastic, for at least 1 hour or overnight. (At this point the dough can be tightly wrapped in plastic and frozen for up to a week.)

Preheat the oven to 350 degrees F.

With floured fingers, press the dough evenly into the bottom and sides of a 9-inch tart pan with a removable bottom. Bake for 35 to 40 minutes, or until the edges are lightly browned. Remove to a rack.

In a small saucepan over low heat, melt the chocolate with the cream. Stir until well combined and remove from the heat to cool slightly. Pour into the baked crust (the crust can be warm) and smooth the surface. At this point the chocolate can be cooled to room temperature, wrapped well and stored for one day at room temperature.

Otherwise, while the ganache is still soft, you can lightly press the cherries stem side down into the surface in concentric circles. Arrange the fruit on top just before serving. Glaze the cherries with melted jelly or dust with confectioners' sugar, if desired. *Serves 6*

Vermont Maple Syrup and Peach Pie

*Although available year-round, most people only think of using maple syrup
on pancakes for a winter's breakfast. This is a shame. Maple syrup has a flavor all its own that
adds a subtle dimension to a homey peach pie. Here the normal double crust is made easier by
rolling the bottom large enough to wrap up and over the fruit filling.*

Flaky Pastry:
2 cups all-purpose flour
3/4 teaspoon salt
1 teaspoon granulated sugar
6 tablespoons cold unsalted butter,
   cut into 1/2-inch pieces
6 tablespoons vegetable shortening
5 to 6 tablespoons ice water

Filling:
6 large peaches (approximately 2 3/4 pounds)
1/4 cup real maple syrup

1/4 cup firmly packed light brown sugar
1/4 teaspoon freshly grated nutmeg
1/2 teaspoon cinnamon
2 tablespoons cornstarch

2 tablespoons unsalted butter,
   cut into 1/2-inch pieces
1 egg, lightly beaten, for brushing
2 teaspoons granulated sugar, for sprinkling
The Best Peach Ice Cream (see p. 82), or a good
   vanilla ice cream, for accompaniment

In a large bowl, combine the flour, salt and sugar. Cut in the butter and shortening with a pastry blender or two knives until the mixture resembles coarse crumbs. Sprinkle with 5 tablespoons of water and toss with a fork to moisten the flour. Gather the dough into a ball, adding another tablespoon of water if necessary. Press the dough into a disk, wrap tightly in plastic wrap and refrigerate 1 hour or overnight.

On a lightly floured surface, roll the dough into a 14-inch circle. Roll the circle up around the rolling pin and carefully transfer it to a 9-inch pie dish. Allow the excess to hang over the rim. Place the dish on a baking sheet and refrigerate while making the filling.

Preheat the oven to 400 degrees F.

Cut the unpeeled peaches into 1/2-inch slices. Toss in a large bowl with the maple syrup, brown sugar, nutmeg, cinnamon and cornstarch. Let stand for 5 minutes and toss again.

Remove the crust from the refrigerator. If the pastry has become too cold, allow it to warm until it is pliable. Pour the filling into the crust, scraping in the juices and any undissolved sugar. Distribute the butter pieces evenly over the filling and then gently fold the overhanging dough up over the peaches. The dough will not cover the filling completely. Brush the pastry with the beaten egg and sprinkle lightly with sugar. Bake in the lower third of the oven for 45 to 50 minutes, or until the top is golden brown and the filling is bubbling. Remove from the oven and let cool for 1 hour. Serve with ice cream. *Serves 6*

Nectarine and Blueberry Cobbler with Brown Sugar Biscuit Crust

From the top, cobblers are supposed to resemble cobblestones with their rough, cobbled texture.
Buried beneath is soft, luscious fruit surrounded by sweetened juices that seep into the biscuit crust.
Use all nectarines, if you choose, or substitute peaches and raspberries.

5 nectarines
1 cup fresh blueberries, washed and stemmed
1/3 cup granulated sugar
1/2 teaspoon ground cinnamon
2 tablespoons fresh lemon juice
1 tablespoon all-purpose flour
Unsalted butter, for greasing

Brown Sugar Biscuit Crust:
1 1/2 cups all-purpose flour
1/3 cup firmly packed light brown sugar

2 teaspoons baking powder
1/2 teaspoon baking soda
1 teaspoon ground cinnamon
1/4 teaspoon salt
6 tablespoons (3/4 stick) unsalted butter
1/3 cup low-fat plain yogurt

1 teaspoon granulated sugar, for sprinkling
Vanilla ice cream or unsweetened whipped cream,
    for topping (optional)

Cut the unpeeled nectarines into 1/2-inch slices. Place them in a medium-sized bowl and toss with the blueberries, sugar, cinnamon, lemon juice and flour. Pour into a buttered 7- by-11-inch or 9-inch-square baking pan.

Preheat the oven to 400 degrees F.

In a food processor fitted with a metal blade, pulse together the flour, brown sugar, baking powder, baking soda, cinnamon and salt. Cut the butter into tablespoon-sized pieces and add to the flour mixture. Process until the mixture resembles coarse meal. Add the yogurt and process just until the dough can be pressed together. Turn out onto a lightly floured sur-face and knead several times by hand. The dough will be stiff.

Pat or roll the dough into an 8-inch circle. Using a 2-inch biscuit cutter, cut out 8 biscuits. Gather the scraps, roll again and cut out 4 more. Place the biscuits, barely touching each other, on top of the fruit. Sprinkle with the sugar and bake in the center of the oven for 35 to 40 minutes until the biscuits have risen and be-come browned around the edges and the fruit has bubbled up between them. Remove from the oven and let cool for 15 minutes. Accom-pany with vanilla ice cream or unsweetened whipped cream, if desired. *Serves 6*

Cherry Vanilla Ice Cream

*If you are a big fan of Bing cherries, you
probably can't find enough ways to use them.
This ice cream is just for you.*

2 cups half-and-half
1 high-quality, moist, supple vanilla bean (available
    at specialty markets)
1 pound dark sweet cherries, pitted
1/2 cup granulated sugar
4 large egg yolks
2 tablespoons kirsch or cherry brandy

In a medium-sized saucepan over high heat,
scald the half-and-half. Remove from heat.
Split the vanilla bean, scrape out the seeds and
add them with the bean to the cream. Cover
and allow the mixture to steep for 1 hour.

Meanwhile, in a medium-sized saucepan,
cook three-quarters of the cherries with the
sugar over moderate heat for 30 minutes, or
until tender. Purée in a food processor or
blender until smooth. You should have 1 cup.

In a small bowl, whisk the yolks until
smooth. Reheat the cream and remove the
vanilla bean. Add one-third of the cream to the
yolks, then pour the mixture back into the
saucepan and cook, stirring constantly, until
the custard is thick enough to coat a spoon.
Using a wire-mesh strainer, strain the custard
into a bowl and stir in the cherry purée and
kirsch. Cover and refrigerate for several hours
or overnight. Freeze in an ice-cream maker
according to the manufacturer's directions,
adding the remaining cherries during the last 5
minutes of freezing. *Makes 1 generous quart*

The Best Peach Ice Cream

*Save your ripest and most aromatic peaches for this
old-fashioned summer treat. Because the peaches are
puréed instead of chopped, you won't bite into an icy
piece of fruit. For variety, add 2 tablespoons minced
candied ginger during the last 5 minutes of freezing.*

2 cups half-and-half
1 high-quality, moist, supple vanilla bean
    (available at specialty markets)
2 pounds (8 to 10) ripe peaches
1 1/2 cups granulated sugar
4 egg yolks
Pinch salt

In a medium-sized saucepan over high heat,
scald the half-and-half. Remove from heat.
Split the vanilla bean, scrape out the seeds and
add them with the bean to the cream. Cover
and allow the mixture to steep for 1 hour.

Meanwhile, peel, pit and slice the peaches
and place them in a large bowl. Toss with 1 cup
of the sugar and allow to macerate for 1 hour,
then purée them in a food processor or blender.

Remove the vanilla bean from the cream
and gently reheat the cream. In a small bowl,
whisk together the yolks, 1/2 cup of sugar and
the salt. Pour a little of the warm cream into the
yolks, then pour the mixture back into the
cream. Cook over moderate heat, stirring constantly, until it is thick enough to coat a spoon.
Remove from the heat, pour the custard
through a wire-mesh strainer into a bowl, stir
in the peach purée and cover and refrigerate for
several hours or overnight. Freeze in an ice-
cream maker according to the manufacturer's
directions. *Makes 1 generous quart*

The Best Peach Ice Cream

Red Plum Sorbet

Curiously, whether you use black-skinned plums with yellow flesh or red-skinned plums
with red flesh, the color of this sorbet seems to be the same. The first time I made it, I expected it to
look like frozen plum jam. But something magical happens in the ice-cream maker. Even with
no cream or eggs, it looks like the pinkest and creamiest of ice creams.

2 pounds red- or black-skinned plums
    (approximately 10)
1 cup granulated sugar
1 tablespoon lemon juice

1 teaspoon pure vanilla extract
Peach halves, for serving (optional)
Mint sprigs, for garnishing (optional)

Halve and pit the plums. Place them in a food processor fitted with a metal blade and purée until smooth; some small shreds of fruit will still be visible. You should have approximately 3 cups.

Pour the purée into a medium-sized saucepan and place over moderate heat. Stir in the sugar and lemon juice. Cook, stirring occasionally, for approximately 15 minutes until the mixture is ruby colored and slightly thickened.

Taste for sweetness and add more sugar if necessary. Remove from the heat and stir in the vanilla. Pour into a bowl and allow the mixture to cool to room temperature. Cover and refrigerate for several hours or overnight. Freeze in an ice-cream maker according to the manufacturer's directions.

To serve, place a rounded scoop in a pitted peach half, if desired, or in a small serving glass and surround with sprigs of mint, if desired.
Makes 3/4 quart

BEVERAGES

Sometimes, on an especially hot day, it takes all the energy you have just to whip up something in the blender that will cool and nourish you. With a few apricots lying in wait in the fruit bowl, an Apricot Yogurt Energy Drink is yours in seconds. In fact, nectarines or peaches or plums or any combination can be substituted for the apricots.

The wonderful stone fruits of summer are ideal for making satisfying blended drinks for all ages. They are easily pitted, don't have to be peeled and are just the right texture. Best of all, you can instantly whip together a healthy breakfast or an afternoon refresher without turning on the stove.

At cocktail time, tropical breezes will follow your every footstep after blending a Nectarine Sunset Punch or a Plum Rum Fizz. A Peach and Banana Daiquiri is a novel twist on an old favorite. If you prefer a nonalcoholic version, simply substitute a compatible fruit juice for the spirits.

Adding slices of fruit to summer drinks can improve looks and add flavor. Float a nectarine slice in homemade lemonade, hook a fat wedge of peach over the rim of a glass of iced tea or infuse a dry white wine with slices of peach or plum. Purée a peach and drop a spoonful into the bottom of a glass of Champagne or ginger ale. Or stir any puréed stone fruit into sparkling water or yogurt for a fruit-enhanced refresher.

Peach and Orange Breakfast Drink

*No need to save this frothy, fruity
drink for breakfast. It also makes an energizing
late afternoon refresher. If you have apricots on
hand, substitute two or three of them for the peach.
Kids will enjoy sipping this healthy milkshake
through a straw. (photograph on page 86)*

1 cup fresh orange juice
1/2 cup nonfat dry milk
1 ripe peach, pitted but unpeeled
1 tablespoon honey
1/2 teaspoon pure vanilla extract
2 ice cubes

Combine all the ingredients in a blender on
high speed until frothy and smooth. Drink at
once. *Serves 1*

Apricot Yogurt Energy Drink

*A great drink for a breakfast on the run or
a late afternoon pick-me-up. It is very palatable,
very low in fat and very nutritious.*

3 apricots
1/2 banana, sliced
1/2 cup low-fat plain yogurt
1/4 cup nonfat dry milk
2 tablespoons honey
2 tablespoons fresh orange juice
1 tablespoon brewer's yeast (optional)
2 ice cubes (optional)

Purée the apricots and banana in a blender on
high speed. Add the yogurt, dry milk, honey
and orange juice. Blend again on high speed
until smooth. Add the yeast and ice cubes,
if desired, and blend to combine. *Makes one
16-ounce serving*

Peach and Banana Daiquiri

As soon as peaches come into season, use your blender to whip up this cocktail.
Its very fruity flavor and golden sunset color make it a soothing summer treat. This drink can
be made deliciously nonalcoholic by substituting apple juice for the rum.

4 ounces dark rum
2 tablespoons superfine granulated sugar
1/2 banana, sliced
2 ripe peaches, unpeeled and sliced

2 tablespoons fresh lemon juice
4 ice cubes
Mint sprigs, for garnish

In a blender, combine the rum, sugar, banana, peaches, lemon juice and ice cubes and blend until smooth. (There will still be little flecks of peach peel visible in the mixture.) Pour into 2 bowl-shaped glasses and garnish with sprigs of fresh mint. *Serves 2*

Nectarine Sunset Punch

Long shadows stretching across a lush green lawn viewed from a white-railed porch—these are the images that come to mind as you sip this quintessential summer drink. Mellow, cool, puréed fruit is extended with a splash of club soda and ice cubes. Life should always be this tranquil.

2 ripe nectarines
3/4 pound wedge of watermelon (weighed with
    rind on)
4 tablespoons granulated sugar
4 teaspoons fresh lime juice

2 cups crushed ice or 12 ice cubes finely chopped
    in blender
4 ounces vodka
1 cup club soda
4 lime wedges, for garnish

Cut the nectarines into quarters and remove the pits. Purée them in the blender and pour the purée into a large pitcher. Cut the watermelon from the rind and remove the seeds. Purée the pulp in the blender until it liquefies and pour it into the pitcher. Vigorously stir in the sugar, lime juice, ice, vodka and soda. Pour into four 10-ounce glasses, rub the rims with lime and garnish with lime wedges. *Makes 4 drinks*

Plum Rum Fizz

*Pale pink and gently frothy, this light and luscious summer cooler tastes awfully good
on a warm evening. It is especially nice when the plums for it come from your own backyard.*

6 tablespoons superfine granulated sugar
3 ounces dark rum
*4 ripe dark-skinned plums, unpeeled and cut
    into chunks*
2 tablespoons fresh lime juice

1/4 cup half-and-half
6 ice cubes
1/4 cup chilled club soda
Sliced plums, for garnish (optional)

In a blender, combine the sugar, rum, plums, lime juice, half-and-half and ice cubes and blend until smooth.

Pour into two 10-ounce glasses and gently stir in the club soda. Garnish with slices of plum, if desired. *Serves 2*

METRIC CONVERSIONS

Liquid Weights

U.S. Measurements	Metric Equivalents
1/4 teaspoon	1.23 ml
1/2 teaspoon	2.5 ml
3/4 teaspoon	3.7 ml
1 teaspoon	5 ml
1 dessertspoon	10 ml
1 tablespoon (3 teaspoons)	15 ml
2 tablespoons (1 ounce)	30 ml
1/4 cup	60 ml
1/3 cup	80 ml
1/2 cup	120 ml
2/3 cup	160 ml
3/4 cup	180 ml
1 cup (8 ounces)	240 ml
2 cups (1 pint)	480 ml
3 cups	720 ml
4 cups (1 quart)	1 litre
4 quarts (1 gallon)	3 3/4 litres

Dry Weights

U.S. Measurements	Metric Equivalents
1/4 ounce	7 grams
1/3 ounce	10 grams
1/2 ounce	14 grams
1 ounce	28 grams
1 1/2 ounces	42 grams
1 3/4 ounces	50 grams
2 ounces	57 grams
3 ounces	85 grams
3 1/2 ounces	100 grams
4 ounces (1/4 pound)	114 grams
6 ounces	170 grams
8 ounces (1/2 pound)	227 grams
9 ounces	250 grams
16 ounces (1 pound)	464 grams

Temperatures

Fahrenheit	Celsius (Centigrade)
32°F (water freezes)	0°C
200°F	95°C
212°F (water boils)	100°C
250°F	120°C
275°F	135°C
300°F (slow oven)	150°C
325°F	160°C
350°F (moderate oven)	175°C
375°F	190°C
400°F (hot oven)	205°C
425°F	220°C
450°F (very hot oven)	230°C
475°F	245°C
500°F (extremely hot oven)	260°C

Length

U.S. Measurements	Metric Equivalents
1/8 inch	3 mm
1/4 inch	6 mm
3/8 inch	1 cm
1/2 inch	1.2 cm
3/4 inch	2 cm
1 inch	2.5 cm
1 1/4 inches	3.1 cm
1 1/2 inches	3.7 cm
2 inches	5 cm
3 inches	7.5 cm
4 inches	10 cm
5 inches	12.5 cm

Approximate Equivalents

1 kilo is slightly more than 2 pounds
1 litre is slightly more than 1 quart
1 meter is slightly over 3 feet
1 centimeter is approximately 3/8 inch

INDEX